Praying the Word

From the Epistles of John

By

L. O. Ovbije

ISBN: 9780985702090

Published by SOIL Foundation, Inc.
P.O. Box 966
Clarkston, GA 30021-0966

DEDICATION

I do whole heartedly dedicate this book to my precious, lovely and forever wonderful parents: my Father the Honorable Chief J. E. Ovbije and my mother Elder Mrs. Margaret Orhe Edokpagha Ovbije, I simply call my father Papa and my mother Mama.
The epistle of John Centre team is Love. I cannot speak, preach or write about love without God not bringing my parents and my upbringing to my attention. I am forever grateful to God for my parents.

They gave me unconditional love, they taught me love, they taught me how to forgive anyone who wrong me, they taught me to never hold a grudge, they believe the best of me, they encouraged me always, they see greatness in me, they never speak negative of each other, or of me. They never speak negative of anyone, they never involve in gossip. They taught me how to relate to ladies, they taught me always put the lady away from the traffic: when walking with a lady on the street, they taught me how to speak(there is a big differences between speaking and talking, when you speak, you say: read St. Mark 11:23, speaking goes with purpose, in speaking there is focus). I remember very well as a child and into my teens, my father would ask me between intervals "what is your target" meaning what is your goal, "yes you are in holiday, but the school did not take books away from you" meaning because school is not in session does not mean you should not be reading, I learned from them, to slow to speak, to never make a statement about a thing without the knowledge of the matter, they taught me to listen, more than talking, I was very aware of the respect and dignity people in the community, in the city I grew up in and in other places, gave to my parents , yes my last name is well known, and I was taught by my parents never to tarnish it, it is like a crown, when I became a Christian, I read in the bible "A good name is rather to be chosen than riches,…" Proverbs 22:1, I thank God I never experience poverty. I do credit them for my education; they taught me the rudiment of education. They prepared the path for me to know God intimately. I am short of words.

There are not enough pages in the world for me to express the love my parents gave to me and my love for them, and all they taught me, also there are not enough pages for me to express my deepest thanks and gratitude to God for my parents.

Father God, I thank you for blessing and ordaining that I should come into this world through this wonderful parents of mine, I am forever grateful to you for my parents, in Jesus name, Amen and Amen and Amen, and a Lot of Amen.

ACKNOWLEDGMENTS

To my wonderful parents, Chief J. E. Ovbije & Mrs. Margaret O. Ovbije, and to my siblings. My father was a man that lived a life that left an excellent and lasting impression on me. Our family knew the meaning of a loving, secure and rich home because of my father's presence. I thank God for the private elementary school at Sapele: Children Nursery School, where I attended. It was there that I encounter God for the first time in prayer in a very early age.

To my precious pastor and his lovely wife, both were strong examples of a man and a woman devoted to God. I was fortunate to have pastor & Mrs. Umukoro, both disciples me. I thank them both for their daily early morning prayer. To the men of God who also impacted my prayer life, W. F. Kumuyi and Benjamin Udi.

Finally to my sweet, precious, wonderful wife Theresa Spearman Ovbije, a woman of God, whom I simply call "sweetie".

"Give Love Much Time, For Love Always Win"

L. O. Ovbije.

"I Am A Lover, Therefore, I Am A Winner"

L. O. Ovbije.

"Give Love A Chance, For Love Will Never Fail You"

L. O. Ovbije.

CHAPTER 1

1 That which was from the beginning, which we have heard, which we have seen with our eyes, which we have looked upon, and our hands have handled, of the Word of life;

Father in the name of Jesus, I thank you for salvation, Father I pray that I never forget the day Jesus Christ came into my heart. Father I thank you for the joy that flood my soul, I have never be the same, change to be like you, Father I pray that I will never forget the simplicity of your grace that led me to accept Jesus Christ into my heart as my Savior and Lord, in Jesus name, Amen.

² (For the life was manifested, and we have seen it, and bear witness, and shew unto you that eternal life, which was with the Father, and was manifested unto us;)

Father in the name of Jesus, I thank you that Christ in me the hope of glory, Father I thank you for your Holy Spirit that dwell in me, that manifest Christ in me and through me daily. Father I thank you that people does see the manifestation of Jesus Christ through me daily, in Jesus name, Amen.

³ That which we have seen and heard declare we unto you, that ye also may have fellowship withus: and truly our fellowship is with the Father, and with his Son Jesus Christ.

Father in Jesus name, I thank you that I am not ashamed of the gospel of Jesus Christ for it is your power unto salvation to every-one that believed, Father I am not ashamed of what you have spoken to me by your Holy Spirit that dwells in me and by your holy word, Father I am not ashamed nor I am intimidated by the devil or anyone, to declare what you will have me to declare, because I am not alone, Father you are always with me, in Jesus name, Amen.

[4] And these things write we unto you, that your joy may be full.

Father in the name of Jesus, I thank you for your written word, Father I thank you for given me access to your written word, Father I thank you that I do read your word daily, I thank you for the joy that your word does produce in me daily, in Jesus name, Amen.

[5] This then is the message which we have heard of him, and declare unto you, that God is light, and in him is no darkness at all.

Father in the name of Jesus, I thank you that you are light; I boldly confess that God is light and God is the One that light me up daily. Father I thank you that there is no darkness in you, I thank you that I do live in you; therefore I do live in purity, in Jesus name, Amen.

[6] If we say that we have fellowship with him, and walk in darkness, we lie, and do not the truth:

Father in Jesus name, I thank you that I do have fellowship with you daily, Father I thank you that I do not walk in darkness, Father I thank you that I am a child of the Light and you are the Light, in Jesus name, Amen.

[7] But if we walk in the light, as he is in the light, we have fellowship one with another, and the blood of Jesus Christ his Son cleanseth us from all sin.

Father in the name of Jesus, I thank you that I do walk in the light and I do have fellowship with other believers in Jesus Christ, Father I thank you for the blood of Jesus Christ which cleanse me from all sin, Father I thank you that I am cleanse from all sin, therefore, Father I thank you that there is no sin in my life because you have cleanse me from all sin by the blood of Jesus Christ, Father I thank you that whenever I miss the mark or sin, I will confess immediately and you are always faithful and just to cleanse me instantaneously, in Jesus name, Amen.

[8] If we say that we have no sin, we deceive ourselves, and the truth is not in us.

Father in the name of Jesus, I pray for the grace to never justify sin or give excuse to sin or for sin, but if I mix the mark, I will confess it and repent of it, you will forgive me and cleanse me from all unrighteousness, I will receive my forgiveness with joy and gratitude, in Jesus name, Amen.

[9] If we confess our sins, he is faithful and just to forgive us our sins, and to cleanse us from all unrighteousness.

Father in the name of Jesus, I thank that whenever I miss the mark or sin, I will come to you and confess it to you, and if it affected anybody, I will also ask them to forgive me. Father after I confess to you and ask for your forgiveness, I will receive my forgiveness and leave with joy, knowing that according to your word I am forgiven and I am cleansed from all unrighteousness, regardless of how I feel. Father I thank you for the precious blood of Jesus Christ that you always use to cleanse me, in Jesus name, Amen.

[10] If we say that we have not sinned, we make him a liar, and his word is not in us.

Father I thank you in Jesus name that your word does abide in me effectually, Father I thank you that whenever I miss the mark, I will not liar against the truth, but I will acknowledge it and confess it to you, Father I pray that I will be quick to repent, and quick to receive forgiveness from you, in Jesus name, Amen.

CHAPTER 2

1 My little children, these things write I unto you, that ye sin not. And if any man sin, we have an advocate with the Father, Jesus Christ the righteous:

Father in Jesus name, I thank you for your word that dwells in me mightily, Father I thank you that I do esteem your word above my necessary food, Father I thank you that your word is sweeter than honey to my taste, Father I thank you that I have no desire to sin, Father I love you dearly, and I have no desire to grieve your Holy Spirit, Father if I sin, I thank you that I can come to you boldly in the name of Jesus to ask you to forgive me, for Jesus Christ is my advocate, and Jesus Christ the righteous ever lives to make intercession for me daily. Father I thank you for Jesus Christ, in Jesus name, Amen.

² And he is the propitiation for our sins: and not for ours only, but also for the sins of the whole world.

Father in Jesus name, I thank you that Jesus Christ is the propitiation for my sins and the sins of the whole world, Father I thank you for Jesus Christ, in Jesus name, Amen.

³ And hereby we do know that we know him, if we keep his commandments.

Father in the name of Jesus, I thank you that I do know you, I thank you that I do keep your commandments, I thank you that you are my very own Father and I am your very own child, in Jesus name, Amen.

⁴ He that saith, I know him, and keepeth not his commandments, is a liar, and the truth is not in him.

Father in Jesus name, I thank you that I do know you, Father I thank you that I do keep your commandments, Father I thank you that I do love you, in Jesus name, Amen.

⁵ But whoso keepeth his word, in him verily is the love of God perfected: hereby know we that we are in him.

Father in Jesus name, I thank you that I do keep your word, Father I thank you that your love is truly perfected in me, Father I thank you that I do know that I am in you, in Jesus name, Amen.

⁶ He that saith he abideth in him ought himself also so to walk, even as he walked.

Father in the name of the Jesus, I thank you that my residence is in Jesus, Father I thank you that I do walk even as Jesus walked, and as he is, so am I in this world, Father I thank you that I am a doer of your word, in Jesus name, Amen.

⁷ Brethren, I write no new commandment unto you, but an old commandment which ye had from the beginning. The old commandment is the word which ye have heard from the beginning.

Father in Jesus name, I thank you that your word is forever settled in heaven, Father I thank you that I do live by your word, Father I pray that I will examine any new teaching in the light of your word, regardless who is doing the teaching, in Jesus name, Amen.

8 Again, a new commandment I write unto you, which thing is true in him and in you: because the darkness is past, and the true light now shineth.

Father in Jesus name, I thank you for the new commandment of love which is in Jesus and in me, Father I thank you that vengeance belongs to you, Father I thank you that love never fails, in Jesus name, Amen.

9 He that saith he is in the light, and hateth his brother, is in darkness even until now.

Father in the name of Jesus, I thank you that I am in the light, Father I thank you that Jesus is the Light, Father I thank you that I am in Christ and I do love the brethren, yes Lord, I do love everyone, in Jesus name, Amen.

10 He that loveth his brother abideth in the light, and there is none occasion of stumbling in him.

Father in Jesus name, I thank you that I do love the brethren, Father I thank you that I do abide in the light, Father I thank you that there is no occasion of stumbling in me, Father I thank you that I am a doer of your word, in Jesus name, Amen.

11 But he that hateth his brother is in darkness, and walketh in darkness, and knoweth not whither he goeth, because that darkness hath blinded his eyes.

Father in the name of Jesus, I thank you that I do love the brethren, Father I thank you that I do know where I am going because I am in Christ and I am walking in the light, in Jesus name, Amen.

¹² I write unto you, little children, because your sins are forgiven you for his name's sake.

Father in the name of Jesus, I thank you for forgiven me all my sins because of the shed blood of Jesus Christ, Father I thank you for the name of Jesus, Father I thank you for the name of Jesus which is above every other name, Father I thank you that whosoever shall call upon the name of Lord Jesus, shall be saved, Father I thank you that I did call upon the name of the Lord Jesus, I thank you that I am saved, in Jesus name, Amen.

¹³ I write unto you, fathers, because ye have known him that is from the beginning. I write unto you, young men, because ye have overcome the wicked one. I write unto you, little children, because ye have known the Father.

Father in the name of Jesus, I thank you for your word to the fathers and spiritual leaders, that they do know Jesus Christ, yes Father, that the fathers and spiritual leaders need never to doubt there salvation. Father I thank you that you assured the younger ones in the Lord that they have overcome the wicked one, yes Lord, I thank you that every young Christians can live victoriously daily, I thank you Father that the Children in the Lord can rejoice because they know you, in Jesus name, Amen.

¹⁴ I have written unto you, fathers, because ye have known him that is from the beginning. I have written unto you, young men, because ye are strong, and the word of God abideth in you, and ye have overcome the wicked one.

Father in the name of Jesus, I thank you for the men who has walk and talk with you for many years, yes those who are still faithful to you because they know you, Father I thank you for the young men that know you and your word do abide in them, therefore, they are strong and have overcome the wicked one, praise God forevermore, in Jesus name, Amen.

15 Love not the world, neither the things that are in the world. If any man love the world, the love of the Father is not in him.

Father in the name of Jesus Christ, I thank you that I am crucified to the world and the world is crucified to me, Father I thank you that I do not love the world neither the things that are in world because your word commanded me not love the world, Father I thank you that I am your obedient child, in Jesus name, Amen.

16 For all that is in the world, the lust of the flesh, and the lust of the eyes, and the pride of life, is not of the Father, but is of the world.

Father in the name of Jesus Christ, I thank you for your Holy Spirit that dwells in me and your grace in my life, that gives me longing for your word and for prayer, Father I thank you that because of your Holy Spirit and your grace in me, I do not have appetite for the things of the word, in Jesus name, Amen.

17 And the world passeth away, and the lust thereof: but he that doeth the will of God abideth for ever.

Father in Jesus name, I thank you that the world and its fashion is passing away, Father I thank you that I am abiding in your Holy Word for ever, in Jesus name, Amen.

18 Little children, it is the last time: and as ye have heard that antichrist shall come, even now are there many antichrists; whereby we know that it is the last time.

Father in the name of Jesus, I thank you for your Holy Spirit does dwell in me, Father I thank you for your Holy Spirit that bring to my attention times and seasons, Father I thank you that I am not ignorant of times and seasons of the move of your Holy Spirit on earth, Father I thank you that your Holy Spirit that dwells in me do bring your word to my attention, and expose the manifestation of the spirit of antichrists, Father I thank you that no matter how the spirit of antichrist try to disguise himself, your Holy Spirit will expose him through your word, Father I thank you for the spirit of discernment, in Jesus name, Amen.

19 They went out from us, but they were not of us; for if they had been of us, they would no doubt have continued with us: but they went out, that they might be made manifest that they were not all of us.

Father in the name of Jesus, I thank you for the spirit of discernment you have given to me, Father I thank you that by their fruits, I will know them, Father I pray that I will walk in your ways, in your word, and in the spirit of discernment, Father I pray that your Holy Spirit will expose religion, religion's spirits, traditions and the traditions of men that makes your word of non-effect, in Jesus matchless name I pray, Amen.

20 But ye have an unction from the Holy One, and ye know all things.

Father in the name of Jesus, I thank you that I do have an unction from the Holy one and I do know all things, Father I thank you that I do not live in the darkness, Father I thank you that I do live in the light of your word, Father I thank you that I am not an Ignorant believer, I thank you that I do have what your word says I have, Father I thank you that your Holy Spirit which dwells in me does teach me all things and He does brings things to my remembrance, in Jesus name, Amen.

²¹ I have not written unto you because ye know not the truth, but because ye know it, and that no lie is of the truth.

Father in the name of Jesus, I thank you that you do believe and trust me that I know the truth, I boldly confess that I do know the truth, Father I thank you that no lie is of the truth, Father I thank you that I do hold to the truth, in Jesus name, Amen.

²² Who is a liar but he that denieth that Jesus is the Christ? He is antichrist, that denieth the Father and the Son.

Father in the name of Jesus, I boldly acknowledge that Jesus is the Christ, Father I thank you that you are my Father, I boldly say so, Father I thank you for telling me that anyone who deny that Jesus is the Christ is antichrist, Father I thank you for revealing to me the spirit that influence those who do deny Jesus Christ, Father I pray that you will open their spiritual eyes, so that they will understand your love and the price Jesus Christ paid for their redemption, in Jesus name, Amen.

²³ Whosoever denieth the Son, the same hath not the Father: he that acknowledgeth the Son hath the Father also.

Father in the name of Jesus, I thank you that you are my very own Father and I am your very own child, I do acknowledge that Jesus Christ is the only person that paid for the sins of the whole world, and that is name is above every name, in Jesus name, Amen.

²⁴ Let that therefore abide in you, which ye have heard from the beginning. If that which ye have heard from the beginning

shall remain in you, ye also shall continue in the Son, and in the Father.

Father in the name of Jesus, I thank you for the simplicity of the gospel, Father I thank you for your grace, Father I thank you for your mercy, Father I thank you that your word does abide in me and I do abide in your word, Father I thank you that I do judge everything by your word, Father I thank you that I am a doer of your word, in Jesus name, Amen.

25 And this is the promise that he hath promised us, even eternal life.

Father in the name of Jesus, I thank you for my salvation, Father I thank you for eternal life, Father I thank you that my hope in you is more than this present life, Father I love you forever, and I know you love me forever, in Jesus name, Amen.

26 These things have I written unto you concerning them that seduce you.

Father in the name of Jesus, I thank you that has I judge everything by your word, false teachers and false teaching cannot hide, your word and the gift of discernment of spirit will expose them, Father I thank you that your word do abide in me and I do abide in your word, therefore, the evil one cannot deceive me, Father I thank you that I do believe that You are who you said You are, I am who You said I am, You have what You said You have, I have what You said I have, You will do what You said You will do, I can do what you said I can do, Father I thank you that I do believe your word, Father let it be to me according to your good word, in Jesus name, Amen.

²⁷ But the anointing which ye have received of him abideth in you, and ye need not that any man teach you: but as the same anointing teacheth you of all things, and is truth, and is no lie, and even as it hath taught you, ye shall abide in him.

Father in the name of Jesus, I thank you for your word, Father I thank you that the anointing that I received from Jesus does abide in me, Father I thank you that the anointing does teach me all things, Father I thank you that the anointing does tell me whenever I hear a false teaching that the teaching is wrong, Father I thank you for the anointing, and he does abide in me forever, in Jesus name, Amen.

²⁸ And now, little children, abide in him; that, when he shall appear, we may have confidence, and not be ashamed before him at his coming.

Father in the name of Jesus, I thank you that your word is truth, Father I thank you that has I live by your word, I am abiding in your word, and has I abide in your word, I am abiding in Christ, Father I pray that I will never be ashamed of your word, no matter what the circumstance may be or where I may be, or who is around me, Father grant me holy boldness to live my life for you daily, without compromise, in Jesus name, Amen.

²⁹ If ye know that he is righteous, ye know that every one that doeth righteousness is born of him.

Father in the name of Jesus, I thank you that you are my Father and I am your child, and I know that you are righteous, I thank you for your Holy Spirit that dwells in me, I thank you that you have given me the spirit of discernment, I also thank you that I do judge all things by your word, Father I thank you that everyone that is born again, is your righteousness in Christ Jesus, in Jesus name, Amen.

CHAPTER 3

1 Behold, what manner of love the Father hath bestowed upon us, that we should be called the sons of God: therefore the world knoweth us not, because it knew him not.

Father in the name of Jesus, I thank you for the manner of love you have put on and in me, Father I thank you for this love which is beyond human understanding, this love which is you, yes, you have come into me, yes, to live in me, that now I can be call your own child, Father of a truth, it is marvelous, since you love me so greatly, I do now love myself, in Jesus name, Amen.

² Beloved, now are we the sons of God, and it doth not yet appear what we shall be: but we know that, when he shall appear, we shall be like him; for we shall see him as he is.

Father in the name of Jesus, I thank you that the moment I accepted Jesus Christ into my heart, that very moment you declared me your child, Father I thank you that right now in this falling world, I am your child and I do represent you in this world, yes Father I am your ambassador in Christ Jesus here on earth, Father I thank you that when Jesus Christ shall appear in the cloud of glory, I shall be like him, for I shall see him as he is, in Jesus name, Amen.

³ And every man that hath this hope in him purifieth himself, even as he is pure.

Father in the name of Jesus, I thank you for your word, Father I thank you that your word does purify me as I act on your word,

Father I thank you that as I do your word, I am cleanse, in Jesus name, Amen.

4 Whosoever committeth sin transgresseth also the law: for sin is the transgression of the law.

Father in Jesus name, I thank you that I do live in the law of love. Father I thank you that as long as I am living in the law of love, I will not sin, because you are Love, Father I pray that I will not move away from the law of love, Father I pray that I will not violate the law of love, but if I do, I pray that I repent immediately, and get back into love commandment. Father I pray that I will live the lifestyle of your kind of love, in Jesus name, Amen.

5 And ye know that he was manifested to take away our sins; and in him is no sin.

Father in Jesus name, I thank you that Jesus Christ came to reconcile me to you, Jesus Christ came that I might have life, and have life more abundantly, Jesus came to destroy the works of the devil, Jesus Christ came to undo on earth that which the devil did on earth, Father I thank that Jesus Christ took away my sins, therefore, I do not have my sins any more, in Jesus name, Amen.

6 Whosoever abideth in him sinneth not: whosoever sinneth hath not seen him, neither known him.

Father in the name of Jesus, I thank you that I do abide in Jesus, therefore, I do not practice sin, I am delivered from practicing sins, if I do sin, I do repent immediately because I am abiding in Jesus and I have no desire to sin, Father I love you and I thank you for Jesus, in Jesus name, Amen.

7 **Little children, let no man deceive you: he that doeth right-eousness is righteous, even as he is righteous.**

Father in the name of Jesus, I thank you that because of your Holy Spirit that dwells in me, I will not let anyone deceive me, I will not receive any teaching in any form about sin consciousness, Father I thank you that I am your righteousness in Christ Jesus, and I do produce the fruit of righteousness, in Jesus name, Amen.

8 **He that committeth sin is of the devil; for the devil sinneth from the beginning. For this purpose the Son of God was mani-fested, that he might destroy the works of the devil.**

Father in the name of Jesus, I thank you that I do not practice sin because I am your very own child and you are my very own Fa-ther, I am your offspring, Father I thank you that Jesus Christ who is my elder brother destroy the works of the devil, and gave me power over all the works of the devil, therefore sins has no domin-ion over me, in Jesus name, Amen.

9 **Whosoever is born of God doth not commit sin; for his seed remaineth in him: and he cannot sin, because he is born of God.**

Father in the name of Jesus, I thank you that I am born of you, Fa-ther I thank you that your seed is in me forever, Father I thank you that I do not practice sin, Father I thank you that whenever I miss the mark, I will repent immediately, Father I thank you that you are my very own Father, and I am your very own child, in Jesus name, Amen.

¹⁰ In this the children of God are manifest, and the children of the devil: whosoever doeth not righteousness is not of God, neither he that loveth not his brother.

Father in the name of Jesus, I thank you that you are my Father and I am your child, Father I thank you that whatsoever is true of you is true of me, like Father, like child. Father I am not ashamed to confess boldly in the presence of religious people that you are my very own Father and I am your very own child. Father because you are Love, I inherited love from you, in fact Father you are great Love, and I am love little. Therefore I love the brethren and everyone, in Jesus name, Amen.

¹¹ For this is the message that ye heard from the beginning, that we should love one another.

Father in the name of Jesus, I thank you that I do love the brethren, Father I thank you, I do walk in love, Father I thank you that I am enjoying walking in love no matter what circumstance I face, I am perfected in your love, I am a child of love, in Jesus name, Amen.

¹² Not as Cain, who was of that wicked one, and slew his brother. And wherefore slew he him? Because his own works were evil, and his brother's righteous.

Father in the name of Jesus, I thank you that you do dwell in me, Father I thank you that I can do no evil, because love does no evil, Father I thank you that your love is perfected in me, in Jesus name, Amen.

¹³ Marvel not, my brethren, if the world hate you.

Father in the name of Jesus, I thank you that I am crucified to the world and the world is crucified to me, Father I thank you that I do not live for the world, Father I thank you that what you say and think about me is what matter to me, not what the world says or thinks about me, in Jesus name, Amen.

[14] We know that we have passed from death unto life, because we love the brethren. He that loveth not his brother abideth in death.

Father in Jesus name, I thank you that you are my very own Father and I am your very own child, Father I thank you that what is true of you is true of me, Father I thank you that you are Love, so I am, Father I thank you that I do love the brethren, Father I thank you that I have passed from death to life because I do love the brethren, Father I thank you that I do not hate anybody because I am born by Love, Father I thank you that I did inherit your love the moment I was born again, in Jesus name, Amen.

[15] Whosoever hateth his brother is a murderer: and ye know that no murderer hath eternal life abiding in him.

Father in Jesus name, I thank you that your love is shed abroad in my heart, Father I thank you that I love me, Father I thank you that I do love the brethren, Father I thank you that I do walk in love, grace and forgiveness, in Jesus name, Amen.

[16] Hereby perceive we the love of God, because he laid down his life for us: and we ought to lay down our lives for the brethren.

Father in Jesus name, I thank you for Jesus Christ, whom you sent to die for me, Father I thank you for your great love that led Jesus Christ to laid down his life for me, Father I thank you that the same love has be shed abroad in my heart, Father I pray that I give that same love the right of way to flow through me to me, to the believers, and to the unbelievers, in Jesus name, Amen.

[17] But whoso hath this world's good, and seeth his brother have need, and shutteth up his bowels of compassion from him, how dwelleth the love of God in him?

Father in Jesus name, I thank you for your word, Father I thank you that according to your divine power you have given me all things that pertain to life and godliness, Father I thank you that you have richly given me all things to enjoy, Father I thank you that every good gift comes from you, Father I thank you that I am what I am by your grace, Father I thank you that I came to this world naked, Father I thank you that all I have come from you primarily, Father I pray that I will share what you have given me with the brethren and the needing, in Jesus name, Amen.

[18] My little children, let us not love in word, neither in tongue; but in deed and in truth.

Father in the name of Jesus, I thank you for your word, Father I thank you for your grace for me not just to love in words only, but to put action to my love for people, Father I am grateful for the grace to put action in love, in Jesus name, Amen.

[19] And hereby we know that we are of the truth, and shall assure our hearts before him.

Father in the name of Jesus, I thank you that I am of the truth because I am your child, your love is shed abroad in my heart, and I do walk in your love, in Jesus name, Amen.

²⁰ For if our heart condemn us, God is greater than our heart, and knoweth all things.

Father in the name of Jesus, I thank you for your Holy Spirit that dwells in me, Father I thank you that I am alive in Christ and I do live in your love, Father I have no desire to miss the mark, but if I do, my heart will notify me, and I will repent immediately without justifying myself, I must decrease and Jesus Christ must increase in my life, in Jesus name, Amen.

²¹ Beloved, if our heart condemn us not, then have we confidence toward God.

Father in Jesus name, I thank you that your Holy Spirit does dwell in me, Father I thank you that your Spirit does speak to my heart, Father I thank you that I do listen to my heart, Father I thank you that if I miss the mark, my heart will tell me and I will repent immediately, Father I thank you that as long as I stay and walk in love, I do have confidence toward you, in Jesus name, Amen.

²² And whatsoever we ask, we receive of him, because we keep his commandments, and do those things that are pleasing in his sight.

Father in the name of Jesus, I thank you that I am a doer of your word, Father I thank you that your word is sweeter than honey to my taste, Father I thank you that I delight in your word, Father I thank you for your promises to me, Father I thank you that I do walk in love, Father I thank you that whatever I ask of you, I will ask in accordance to your word, and I know my petition is grant when I ask, because I am abiding in your word, in Jesus name, Amen.

23 And this is his commandment, That we should believe on the name of his Son Jesus Christ, and love one another, as he gave us commandment.

Father in the name of Jesus, I thank you that I do believe on the name of Jesus, Father I thank you that your love is shred abroad in my heart and I do love the brethren, yes the Christians, just as you have commanded me to, I also love the unbelievers with your kind of love, in Jesus name, Amen.

24 And he that keepeth his commandments dwelleth in him, and he in him. And hereby we know that he abideth in us, by the Spirit which he hath given us.

Father in the name of Jesus, I thank you that I am a doer of your word, Father I thank you that I do keep your word, Father I thank you that I do keep your word in my heart that I might not sin against thee, Father I thank you that I am your dwelling place and your Spirit is in me forever, in Jesus name, Amen.

CHAPTER 4

1 Beloved, believe not every spirit, but try the spirits whether they are of God: because many false prophets are gone out into the world.

Father in the name of Jesus, I thank you for your word, Father I thank you that your word does abide in me and I do abide in your word, Father I thank you that I do know the Truth, Father I thank you that by your word and through your word, I do try every spirit, Father I also thank you for the gift of discernment you have given me, in Jesus name, Amen.

2 Hereby know ye the Spirit of God: Every spirit that confesseth that Jesus Christ is come in the flesh is of God:

Father in the name of Jesus, I thank you that Jesus Christ came in the flesh, Father I thank you that Jesus Christ in the flesh to destroy the works of the devil and to restore me back to you, Father I boldly confess to the world, to religious people, and to the devil that Jesus Christ came in the flesh, Father I thank you that I am your child, in Jesus name, Amen.

3 And every spirit that confesseth not that Jesus Christ is come in the flesh is not of God: and this is that spirit of antichrist, whereof ye have heard that it should come; and even now already is it in the world.

Father in Jesus name, I thank you that Jesus Christ came in the flesh, Father I thank you that your word is forever settled, Father I thank you that anyone who do not believe and confess that Jesus Christ came in the flesh is not born again, Father I thank you that I do believe that Jesus Christ came in the flesh and I do boldly confess with my mouth Jesus Christ came in the flesh, in Jesus name, Amen.

4 Ye are of God, little children, and have overcome them: because greater is he that is in you, than he that is in the world.

Father in the name of Jesus, I thank you that I am your child, Father I thank you that because I am born of you, I have overcome the world, Father I thank you that I am led by your Spirit, and not by my feeling, Father I thank you that you that is in me is greater than the evil one that is in the world, Father I thank you that I am not afraid of the evil one because Jesus Christ defeated the evil one and gave me power over the evil one, in Jesus name, Amen.

5 They are of the world: therefore speak they of the world, and the world heareth them.

Father in the name of Jesus, I thank you for your word, Father I thank you that your word is truth, Father I thank you for sanctify me by your word, Father I thank you for setting me apart by your word, Father I thank you that I am in the world but not of the world, Father I thank you that I do not speak like the unbelievers speaks, Father I thank you that I do use your word to governor my word, in Jesus name, Amen.

6 We are of God: he that knoweth God heareth us; he that is not of God heareth not us. Hereby know we the spirit of truth, and the spirit of error.

Father in the name of Jesus, I thank you that you are my Father, Father I thank you that you have taken your right place in my life as a Father, Father I thank you that I do speak your word continually, Father I thank you that anyone who is born again does listen to your word that comes out of my mouth, in Jesus name, Amen.

7 Beloved, let us love one another: for love is of God; and every one that loveth is born of God, and knoweth God.

Father in the name of Jesus, I thank you that your love is shed abroad in the heart of every believer in Jesus Christ, I pray that your kind of love will manifest among those of us who profess to be Christian, Father I pray that we will not be ashamed to walk in your kind of love towards one another, Father I pray that we will consciously and boldly love one another, that the unbelievers may know that we are Jesus Christ disciples, in Jesus name, Amen.

8 He that loveth not knoweth not God; for God is love.

Father in the name of Jesus, I thank you that you are love, Father I thank you that your love has been shed abroad in my heart, Father I thank you that I am born of you, Father I thank you that I inherit love from you, Father I thank you that I am a lover, Father I thank you that I do love everybody regardless of their appearance, in Jesus name, Amen.

9 In this was manifested the love of God toward us, because that God sent his only begotten Son into the world, that we might live through him.

Father in the name of Jesus, I thank you that you sent Jesus Christ to the world because you love the world, Father I thank you that you love people, yes glory to your holy name, Father I thank you that you love me, Father I thank you that you sent Jesus Christ to die for me because you love me, Father I thank you for this great love from you to me, Father I thank you that I am living in your great love regardless of religious teachings, in the name of Jesus Christ of Nazareth adjourn my feelings to abide in this great love of God Almighty, in Jesus name, Amen.

[10] Herein is love, not that we loved God, but that he loved us, and sent his Son to be the propitiation for our sins.

Father in the name of Jesus, I thank you for your love for me and for your love for the world, Father I thank you that because you love me, you sent Jesus Christ to pay the ransom for my soul, Father I thank you for the manifestation of your great love for me by sending Jesus Christ to me, Father I love you, in Jesus name, Amen.

[11] Beloved, if God so loved us, we ought also to love one another.

Father in Jesus name, I thank you for your word, Father I thank you that you love me, Father I thank you that since you love me, I do love me, Father I thank you that since I love me, I do love the brethren and I do love everyone, in Jesus name, Amen.

[12] No man hath seen God at any time. If we love one another, God dwelleth in us, and his love is perfected in us.

Father in the name of Jesus, I thank you that you are my very own Father and I am your very own child, Father I thank you that your love has been shed abroad in my heart by your Holy Spirit, Father I thank you that I love me, and I do love the brethren, Father I thank you that you do live in me, in Jesus name, Amen.

¹³ Hereby know we that we dwell in him, and he in us, because he hath given us of his Spirit.

Father in the name of Jesus, I thank you that you gave your Holy Spirit to me when I accepted Jesus Christ into my heart, Father I thank you for your Holy Spirit that abide with me forever, Father I thank you that Christ in me the hope of glory, I thank you that in you I live, move, and have my being, Father I thank you that you are my very own Father and I am your very own child, in Jesus name, Amen.

¹⁴ And we have seen and do testify that the Father sent the Son to be the Saviour of the world.

Father in the name of Jesus, I thank you for your word, Father I thank you that you did send your Son whose name is Jesus into the world to save the world, Father I thank you that I have accepted Jesus Christ as my Saviour, Father I thank you that your Spirit does bear witness with my spirit that I am your child, Father I thank you that my spirit does bear witness and testify that Jesus is your Son, in Jesus name, Amen.

¹⁵ Whosoever shall confess that Jesus is the Son of God, God dwelleth in him, and he in God.

Father in the name of Jesus, I thank you for Jesus Christ, Father I boldly believe with my own heart and I boldly confess with my own mouth that Jesus is your Son, Father I thank you and I boldly acknowledge that you do live in me, in Jesus name, Amen.

¹⁶ And we have known and believed the love that God hath to us. God is love; and he that dwelleth in love dwelleth in God, and God in him.

Father in Jesus name, I thank you that I do believe the love you have for me, Father I thank you that I do believe that you love me, Father thank you that you are love, Father I thank you that I am your child of love, Father I thank you that I do live in your love, Father I thank you that I will not allow religion to contaminate your love for me, Father I thank you that I will not allow what I do or did not do to contaminate your love for me, Father I thank you that I do not have to perform in any way for your love to continue to energize me daily, in Jesus name, Amen.

[17] Herein is our love made perfect, that we may have boldness in the day of judgment: because as he is, so are we in this world.

Father in the name of Jesus, I thank you that whatever is true of you is true of me because you are my Father and I am your child, Father I thank you that I am your offspring, Father I thank you that you have made my love perfect and I do have bold access to you, Father I thank you that I am your child and I do have boldness in the day of judgment: because as you are, so I am in this world, in Jesus name, Amen.

[18] There is no fear in love; but perfect love casteth out fear: because fear hath torment. He that feareth is not made perfect in love.

Father in the name of Jesus, I thank you that you did not give me the spirit of fear, but you have given me the spirit of power, and of love, and of a sound mind, Father you tell me in your word again and again fear not, that is I should not fear neither be afraid, Father I thank you that I am your obedient child therefore, I will not fear neither be afraid, Father I thank you that I am perfected in love, in Jesus name, Amen.

¹⁹ We love him, because he first loved us.

Father in the name of Jesus, I thank you that you commanded your love towards me when you sent Jesus Christ to the world to die for my sins, Father you love me greatly that you refused to leave me to perish in my sin, but your love compared you to send Jesus Christ to redeem me from my sin, Father I thank you that greater love hath no man than this, that a man lay down his life for his friends, Lord Jesus I thank you for you did laid down your life for me, Father I thank you for your love that is shed abroad in my heart by your Holy Spirit, Father I thank you that now that your love is in my heart, I can love you with the same love you put in my heart, Father I thank you that I can now love me, myself, and people with the same love you put in my heart, in Jesus name, Amen.

²⁰ If a man say, I love God, and hateth his brother, he is a liar: for he that loveth not his brother whom he hath seen, how can he love God whom he hath not seen?

Father in the name of Jesus, I thank you that your love has been shed abroad in my heart by your Holy Spirit, Father I thank you that I love me, and I love the brethren, Father I thank you that I do love the brethren as myself, Father I thank you that your love does manifest in me and through me, therefore, I do not hate anyone, Father in the name of Jesus I boldly confess that I refuse to hate anybody for your love is in me mightily, in Jesus name, Amen.

²¹ And this commandment have we from him, That he who loveth God love his brother also.

Father in the name of Jesus, I thank you for your love that has been shed abroad in my heart by your Holy Spirit which you gave to me in salvation, Father I thank you that I love you forever, Father I thank you for your commandment of love, Father I thank you that I love me, and I love the brethren, in Jesus name, Amen.

CHAPTER 5

1 Whosoever believeth that Jesus is the Christ is born of God: and every one that loveth him that begat loveth him also that is begotten of him.

Father in the name of Jesus, I thank you that I do believe Jesus is the Christ, Father I thank you that I am born of you, Father I thank you that I do love Jesus Christ, Father I thank you that I love you, in Jesus name, Amen.

[2] By this we know that we love the children of God, when we love God, and keep his commandments.

Father in the name of Jesus, I thank you for your commandments, Father I thank you that your commandments are not grievous, I thank you that you gave the commandments to me for my own good, Father I thank you that as I live and walk in your love, I do fulfil all the commandments, Father I thank you that I do love all your children which I am one of them, in Jesus name, Amen.

[3] For this is the love of God, that we keep his commandments: and his commandments are not grievous.

Father in the name of Jesus, I thank you that you are my very own Father, and I am your very own child, Father I thank you that you are a righteous and just Father, I thank you that you will not tell me to do what you have not equip me to do, or that you will not enable me to do, Father I thank you that according to your word, I can do all things through Christ who strengtheneth me, Father I say be it unto me according to your word, I am doer of your word, I am a winner, I am a world overcomer, in Jesus name, Amen.

4 For whatsoever is born of God overcometh the world: and this is the victory that overcometh the world, even our faith.

Father in the name of Jesus, I thank you that I am born of you, Father I thank you that I am world overcomer, Father I thank you that I am crucify to the world and the world is crucify to me, Father I take on the shield of faith to quench all the firing darts of the devil, Father I thank you that my faith is in Jesus Christ and his finished works, my faith is in your word, my faith is in your Holy Spirit that dwell in me, my faith is in the gifts of the Spirit in me, my faith is in the fruit of the Spirit in me, these gives me the audacity to overcome the world, in Jesus name, Amen.

5 Who is he that overcometh the world, but he that believeth that Jesus is the Son of God?

Father in the name of Jesus, I thank you that I do believe that Jesus is your Son. Father I thank you that I am a believer in Jesus Christ. Father I thank you that I am world overcomer, in Jesus name, Amen.

6 This is he that came by water and blood, even Jesus Christ; not by water only, but by water and blood. And it is the Spirit that beareth witness, because the Spirit is truth.

Father in the name of Jesus, I thank you that by your grace I do believe that Jesus Christ came by water and blood, Father I thank you that my spirit bears witness that Jesus Christ came by water and blood, in Jesus name, Amen.

7 **For there are three that bear record in heaven, the Father, the Word, and the Holy Ghost: and these three are one.**

Father in the name of Jesus, I thank you that you, the Word and the Holy Ghost are one. Father I thank you that you were manifested as the Word, and the Word became flesh, that flesh which is Jesus Christ on earth, show what your will is on earth, Jesus Christ died and rose up from the grave and ascended up to heaven and he is sitting at your right hand interceding for me always, Father I thank you for sending the Holy Ghost to me on earth, Father I thank you that because I accepted Jesus Christ into my heart, the Holy Ghost now lives in me, Father I thank you for salvation and the indwelling of the Holy Ghost, I thank you that the Holy Ghost is with me forever, in Jesus name, Amen.

8 **And there are three that bear witness in earth, the Spirit, and the water, and the blood: and these three agree in one.**

Father in the name of Jesus, I thank you for your Holy Spirit that dwells in me, Father I thank you for your word that abide in me and I do abide in your word, Father I thank you for the blood of Jesus Christ that you used to redeem me and that you do use to cleanse me daily, Father I am grateful to you forever, in Jesus name, Amen.

9 **If we receive the witness of men, the witness of God is greater: for this is the witness of God which he hath testified of his Son.**

Father in the name of Jesus, I thank you that your witness is greater than the witness of men, therefore, Father I will obey you rather than men, in Jesus name, Amen.

10 He that believeth on the Son of God hath the witness in himself: he that believeth not God hath made him a liar; because he believeth not the record that God gave of his Son.

Father in the name of Jesus, I thank you that you did revealed and still revealing your Son Jesus Christ to me by your Holy Spirit, Father I thank you that I do believe Jesus Christ is your Son, Father I thank you that your Holy Spirit does bear witness with my Spirit that Jesus Christ is your Son and that I am redeem, yes I am saved, in Jesus name, Amen.

11 And this is the record, that God hath given to us eternal life, and this life is in his Son.

Father in the name of Jesus, I thank you for Jesus Christ who is my Saviour and Lord, Father I have accepted Jesus Christ into my heart, Father I thank you that Christ is in me, Father I thank you that because I accepted Jesus Christ into my life, I do have eternal life, in Jesus name, Amen.

12 He that hath the Son hath life; and he that hath not the Son of God hath not life.

Father in the name of Jesus, I thank you that I do have life because I have accepted Jesus Christ into my heart, Father I thank you that I do have your Son Jesus Christ in my heart, Father I pray for those who have not accept your Son Jesus Christ, that your grace and mercy will visit them, the Lord of the harvest, I pray you will send many labourers to them to sow your word of life into their hearts, Father I thank you for giving the increase of souls to your Kingdom, in Jesus name I pray, Amen.

¹³ These things have I written unto you that believe on the name of the Son of God; that ye may know that ye have eternal life, and that ye may believe on the name of the Son of God.

Father in the name of Jesus, I thank you for your written word to me, Father I thank you that your word was written for me, that I may have a personal intimate relationship with you, Father I thank you that your word said I should search the scriptures, yes daily, I should give attendances to the reading of your word, I should meditate in your word day and night, I should be doer of your word and not a hearer only, Father I thank you that I do believe that Jesus Christ is your Son, and I have accepted Jesus Christ into my heart as my Lord and Saviour, and I do confess Jesus Christ with my own mouth that He is my Lord and Saviour, Father I thank you that I do possess eternal life in this present world because Christ is in me, and I do believe on the name of Jesus Christ, in Jesus name I pray, Amen.

¹⁴ And this is the confidence that we have in him, that, if we ask any thing according to his will, he heareth us:

Father in the name of Jesus, I thank you for your will, Father I thank you for your holy word, Father I thank you that your holy word is your written will, Father in the name of Jesus I thank you that you will not contradict your written word. Father I thank you that you are not keeping your will from me, but because I am your child you desire for me to know your will, Father I thank you that it is my uttermost responsibility to read your written will for me, Father I pray that I will not give the responsibility of my reading your written word daily to someone else, I pray by your grace that I will make the reading of your word, meditation, and prayer my daily priority, Father I thank you that your word does produce confidence in me. Father I thank you for inviting me to come boldly to your throne of grace, Father I thank you that it is the throne of grace, not the throne of judgment, but the throne of grace, so that I can obtain mercy and find grace to help in time of need, and I do have the confidence in you my Father that if I ask anything according to your will, you will hear me, and because you hear me , my petition is grant by you, in Jesus name I pray, Amen.

[15] And if we know that he hear us, whatsoever we ask, we know that we have the petitions that we desired of him.

Father in the name of Jesus, I thank you that your word said, ask and you shall receive, seek and you shall find, knock and it shall be open unto you, for everyone that ask, receive, for everyone that seek, find, and to everyone that knock, it shall be open, Father I thank you for all your precious promises you have given to me, because you love me very dearly, and I whole heartedly believe you do, Father I thank you that the evil one cannot make me to question your love for me, or doubt your love for me, Father I thank you that the evil one knows that the major demonstration of your love for me, was when you sent Jesus Christ to me, and you put my sins upon Jesus Christ, who died in my place, then you declared me righteous, Father I thank you for your Holy Spirit who revealed this matter to me. Father I thank you that you have richly given me all things to enjoy, Father I thank you that you are my very own Father and I am your very own child, Father I thank you that whatever I ask according to your will, you do hear me, and you do grant me my petitions, therefore, I receive the answer, in Jesus name I pray, Amen.

[16] If any man see his brother sin a sin which is not unto death, he shall ask, and he shall give him life for them that sin not unto death. There is a sin unto death: I do not say that he shall pray for it.

Father in the name of Jesus, I thank you for your amazing grace, the grace that is beyond explanation, Father I pray that when I see a Christian sin, that I will pray for the Christian, and not to involve in gossip. I pray that I will walk in love and always remember that I stand by grace, Father I thank you for your grace in my life, and for your grace through the power of your Holy Spirit that keep me daily from sin, in Jesus name, Amen.

[17] All unrighteousness is sin: and there is a sin not unto death.

Father in the name of Jesus, I thank you for redemption, I thank you for my salvation, Father I thank you that I do judge everything by your word, Father I thank you that I do not practice sin, Father I thank you that whenever I miss the mark, I repent immediately by asking for your forgiveness, and if anybody is involved that I need to ask for forgiveness, I ask that individual for forgiveness, and I will receive my forgiveness, and I will leave pure and joyfully, in Jesus name, Amen.

[18] We know that whosoever is born of God sinneth not; but he that is begotten of God keepeth himself, and that wicked one toucheth him not.

Father in the name of Jesus, I thank you that I am born of you, Father I thank you that because I am born of you and your seed abide in me, I do not practice sin nor live in sin. Yes Lord I do not live a sinful life, Father I thank you that I do keep myself in your love and the wicked one cannot touch me, Father I thank you that I am the apple of your eyes, Father I thank you that I am inscribe in the palm of your hands, Father I thank you that you are my very own Father, and I am your very own child, in Jesus name, Amen.

¹⁹ And we know that we are of God, and the whole world lieth in wickedness.

Father in the name of Jesus, I thank you that I am of you, for in Christ Jesus you begotten me, I am a new creature in Christ Jesus. I am in the light and the world is in darkness, in Jesus name, Amen.

²⁰ And we know that the Son of God is come, and hath given us an understanding, that we may know him that is true, and we are in him that is true, even in his Son Jesus Christ. This is the true God, and eternal life.

Father in the name of Jesus, I thank you that no one can come to Jesus Christ except you draw the person by your Holy Spirit to Jesus Christ. Father I thank you for Jesus Christ who by your Holy Spirit reveal you to me. Father I believe and I know you are the True God and Jesus Christ is your Son, in Jesus name, Amen.

²¹ Little children, keep yourselves from idols. Amen.

Father in the name of Jesus, I thank you for the indwelling of your Holy Spirit in me, Father I thank you that you alone is my God, and you are my very own Father and I am your very own child, Father I thank you that you are above everything in my life, in the name of Jesus, Amen.

2 JOHN

[1] The elder unto the elect lady and her children, whom I love in the truth; and not I only, but also all they that have known the truth;

Father in the name of Jesus, I thank you for your love for me, Father I thank you for your love for those I have led to the saving knowledge of Jesus Christ, Father I thank you for your love for my children, in Jesus name, Amen.

[2] For the truth's sake, which dwelleth in us, and shall be with us for ever.

Father in the name of Jesus, I thank you that the truth does dwell in me, Father I thank you that the truth is in me forever, Father in the name of Jesus, I boldly confess to the world and to the evil one that the truth is in me, in Jesus name, Amen.

[3] Grace be with you, mercy, and peace, from God the Father, and from the Lord Jesus Christ, the Son of the Father, in truth and love.

Father in the name of Jesus, I thank you for your grace, I thank you for your mercy, I thank you for your peace. Father in the name of Jesus, I receive into my life and my daily walk, grace, mercy and peace that comes only from you and my Lord Jesus Christ, in Jesus name, Amen.

4 **I rejoiced greatly that I found of thy children walking in truth, as we have received a commandment from the Father.**

Father in the name of Jesus, I thank you for those that I have introduced to Jesus Christ and those that I disciple, I thank you for my children and my children in the Lord, Father I rejoice in their steadfastness in Christ Jesus, Father I thank you for your goodness towards them and their love ones, in Christ they stand, in Jesus name, Amen.

5 **And now I beseech thee, lady, not as though I wrote a new commandment unto thee, but that which we had from the beginning, that we love one another.**

Father in the name of Jesus, I thank you for your precious word, Father I thank you that your word teaches me to love, Father I thank you that I inherited your love, Father I thank you that you are Love, Father I thank you that I am a lover, in Jesus name, Amen.

6 **And this is love, that we walk after his commandments. This is the commandment, That, as ye have heard from the beginning, ye should walk in it.**

Father in Jesus name, I thank you that your commandment is not grievous, Father I thank you that all your commandments are fulfill in your commandment of love, Father I thank you that I am a lover and I do walk in love, in Jesus name, Amen.

7 **For many deceivers are entered into the world, who confess not that Jesus Christ is come in the flesh. This is a deceiver and an antichrist.**

Father in the name of Jesus, I thank you that I do believe that Jesus Christ came in the flesh, I boldly confess that Jesus Christ came in the flesh, Father I thank you that I cannot be deceive, because your Spirit is in me forever, your word does abide in me and I do abide in your word, in Jesus name, Amen.

⁸ Look to yourselves, that we lose not those things which we have wrought, but that we receive a full reward.

Father in the name of Jesus, I pray that we that are believers in Christ, will exhort and encourage those that we have led to Christ to be steadfast in the word of the Lord, to be unmovable, and to always abide in the things of God, in Jesus name, Amen.

⁹ Whosoever transgresseth, and abideth not in the doctrine of Christ, hath not God. He that abideth in the doctrine of Christ, he hath both the Father and the Son.

Father in the name of Jesus, I thank you that your word is abiding in me and I am abiding in your word, Father I thank you that I do delight in acting on your word, Father I thank you that I am abiding in the doctrine of Christ, in Jesus name, Amen.

¹⁰ If there come any unto you, and bring not this doctrine, receive him not into your house, neither bid him God speed:

Father in the name of Jesus, I thank you that there is no other foundation but Jesus Christ, Father I thank you that Jesus Christ is the only True Foundation, Father I thank you that there is none other name under heaven given among men, whereby we must be saved. Father I thank you that SALVATION is ONLY in JESUS CHRIST, Father I thank you that I will not receive anybody that come to me with another name, Father I thank you that I will not bid them God speed, in Jesus name, Amen.

¹¹ For he that biddeth him God speed is partaker of his evil deeds.

Father in the name of Jesus, I thank you that I am a doer of your word, Father I thank you that by your grace I will not bid anyone God speed that bring any false teach or false doctrine to me, I will not allow such one into my house, for my house is your house, in Jesus name, Amen.

¹² Having many things to write unto you, I would not write with paper and ink: but I trust to come unto you, and speak face to face, that our joy may be full.

Father in Jesus name, I thank you for your word, Father I thank you that you told us in your word that we should communicate with each other, to encourage one another, Father I pray that I will communicate your love to others daily, in Jesus name, Amen.

¹³ The children of thy elect sister greet thee. Amen.

Father in the name of Jesus, I thank you for those I have led to Christ, Father I thank you for those I will be leading to Christ, I thank you for your Holy Spirit that reveal Jesus Christ to people through me., Father I am grateful, in Jesus name, Amen.

3 JOHN

¹ The elder unto the wellbeloved Gaius, whom I love in the truth.

Father in the name of Jesus, I thank you for your love for me, Father I thank you that you are the Truth, Father I thank you that I do abide in the Truth, in Jesus name, Amen.

² Beloved, I wish above all things that thou mayest prosper and be in health, even as thy soul prospereth.

Father in the name of Jesus, I thank you for your word, Father I thank you that you made the heavens and the earth, and the things therein, Father I thank you that silvers and gold belongs to you, Father I thank you that every beast of the forest is yours, and the cattle upon a thousand hills is yours, Father of a truth, your resources are unsearchable, Father I thank you that you are my very own Father and I am your very own child, Father I thank you that your will for me is prosperity, yes Father, your will for me above all things is that I prosper and be in health, even as my soul prosper. Father I take you at your word, Father I will not let the devil use religious people to talk me out of your will for me, in the name of Jesus I refuse to be poor, Father you said, you will not withhold any good thing from me, my Father, you blessed me with a wonderful earthly father, the greatest earthly father, my heavenly Father, I know you will not do less than my earthly father, Father I thank you that you are my Shepherd, I shall not lack, Father you said, I should meditate in your word day and night, that I should not turn to the right or to the left, and I will make my way prosper, and I will have good success, Father I thank you that I do meditate in your word day and night, and I do not turn to the right or to the left, yes I am focus on the word of my God, Yes I do make my way prosper and I do have good success, Father I thank you for blessing my coming in and blessing my going out, Father I thank you, that according to your word, riches are in my house, Father I say yes, let it be to me according to your word, In Jesus name I boldly confess I am rich, I boldly confess my Father God is supplying all my needs, I boldly confess my Father has given me all things pertaining to life and godliness, I boldly confess my Father has given me all things to enjoy, in Jesus name, Amen.

[3] For I rejoiced greatly, when the brethren came and testified of the truth that is in thee, even as thou walkest in the truth.

Father in the name of Jesus, I thank you for my salvation, Father I thank you that by your grace, I can say I am not of those that fall away, Father I thank you that I am abiding in your word, Father I thank you that I do not draw back, Father I thank you that I cannot be deceive because I am abiding in you, in Jesus name, Amen.

[4] I have no greater joy than to hear that my children walk in truth.

Father in the name of Jesus, I thank you that you commanded me to preach the gospel because I am a believer, Father I thank you for the privilege for me to be co-labourer with you in the sharing of the gospel with unbelievers, Father I thank you for those that came to know Jesus Christ as their Lord and Saviour, I thank you for those of them that are still walking with the Master, in Jesus name, Amen.

⁵ Beloved, thou doest faithfully whatsoever thou doest to the brethren, and to strangers;

Father in the name of Jesus, I thank you for your word, Father I thank you for your faithfulness, Father I thank you for the grace to be faithful in words and in deeds, Father I thank you that I will be faithful in all my dealing with those that are saved and those that are not saved, in Jesus name, Amen.

⁶ Which have borne witness of thy charity before the church: whom if thou bring forward on their journey after a godly sort, thou shalt do well:

Father in the name of Jesus, I thank you for your love for me, Father I pray that your love wish is shed abroad in my heart will manifest through me to people, Father I pray that whenever people speaks about me, that they will speak of my love for you and for people, in Jesus name, Amen.

⁷ Because that for his name's sake they went forth, taking nothing of the Gentiles.

Father in the name of Jesus, I thank you for those who are preaching the word of my Lord and Saviour Jesus Christ, Father I pray that you provide for them, Father I pray also for those that are receiving the message, that you will provide for them and use them to sow seeds into the life of the ministers, in Jesus name, Amen.

⁸ We therefore ought to receive such, that we might be fellowhelpers to the truth.

Father in the name of Jesus, I pray that the Christians that are not in the mission field will support the Christians that are in the mission field, Father I pray that you will enlighten the eyes of the understanding of those Christians that are not in the mission field that they will know that you want them not only support their local Church but to personally look for minister in the mission field to support, in Jesus name, Amen.

⁹ I wrote unto the church: but Diotrephes, who loveth to have the preeminence among them, receiveth us not.

Father in the name of Jesus, I thank you that you know and I know that there is a lot of power struggle in many local Churches, many of your Children are being enslave to one group or the other, many of your children do not know that they can have personal relationship with you, many do not know that whom the Son set free is free indeed, many saved people still entangle with the yoke of bondage, Father I pray you will arise and set your children free again, in Jesus name, Amen.

¹⁰ Wherefore, if I come, I will remember his deeds which he doeth, prating against us with malicious words: and not content therewith, neither doth he himself receive the brethren, and forbiddeth them that would, and casteth them out of the church.

Father in the name of Jesus, I thank you that vengeance belongs to you, Father I pray for those that the devil is using to hinder the gospel that you will visit them as you visited Saul on the road to Damascus, Father I pray that you will remove spiritual blindness from their eyes, in Jesus name, Amen.

¹¹ Beloved, follow not that which is evil, but that which is good. He that doeth good is of God: but he that doeth evil hath not seen God.

Father in the name of Jesus, I thank you that your word said to me to look unto Jesus who is the author and finisher of my faith, Father I thank you that I am looking unto Jesus Christ, Father I thank you for the example Jesus Christ left for me, the example I will follow, in Jesus name, Amen.

12 Demetrius hath good report of all men, and of the truth itself: yea, and we also bear record; and ye know that our record is true.

Father in the name of Jesus, I pray that I will have good report of all men, Father I pray that my everyday living among believers and unbelievers will bring glory to you, Father I thank you for the grace for me not to compromise your word, in Jesus name, Amen.

13 I had many things to write, but I will not with ink and pen write unto thee:

Father in the name of Jesus, I thank you for your written word, Father I pray that as I read, mediate, and study your written word, that I will also be spiritually sensitive to the voice of your Holy Spirit, in Jesus name, Amen.

14 But I trust I shall shortly see thee, and we shall speak face to face. Peace be to thee. Our friends salute thee. Greet the friends by name.

Father in the name of Jesus, I thank you for the grace and privilege to share the gospel of Jesus Christ, Father I pray that we that minister the gospel will encourage one another regardless of our denomination affiliation, in Jesus name, Amen.

SOIL Foundation, Inc.

Publication

Books

All Day God

Praying the Word From the Book of Timothy

Praying the Word From the Book of Ephesians

Resurrection from the Flood

Coaching to Completion

Praying the Word From the Epistle of John

Tracts:

5 Things God wants you to know

Love Yourself